FREE LANCE
AND THE
DRAGON'S HOARD

PAUL STEWART is the author of many books for children including The Wakening. In recent years he has collaborated extensively with illustrator Chris Riddell, most notably on the hugely successful series *The Edge Chronicles*, *The Blobheads* series and *Muddle Earth*. He lives in Brighton with his wife and two children.

CHRIS RIDDELL is the acclaimed cartoonist for The Observer newspaper and the highly successful illustrator of a wide variety of books for children including Kate Greenaway Medal winner *Pirate Diary*. He also lives in Brighton with his wife and three children.

In 2004 Paul and Chris won the Smarties Gold Award in the 6-8 category for *Fergus Crane*.

FREE LANCE
AND THE
DRAGON'S HOARD

Paul Stewart
Chris Riddell

Hodder
Children's
Books

a division of Hodder Headline Limited

PS – For Stephen
CR – For Jack

Text & Illustrations copyright © 2005 Paul Stewart & Chris Riddell

Published in Great Britain in 2005
by Hodder Children's Books.

The right of Paul Stewart and Chris Riddell to be identified as the author
and illustrator of this work has been asserted by them in accordance
with the Copyright, Designs and Patents Act 1988.

Consultant: Wendy Cooling
Designer: Jane Hawkins

A catalogue record for this book is available from the British Library.

ISBN 034087404X

Printed and bound at Clays Ltd, St Ives plc

The paper used in this book is a natural recyclable product made from
wood grown in sustainable forests. The hardcover board is recycled.

Hodder Children's Books
A division of Hodder Headline Limited
338 Euston Road, London NW1 3BH

1

'Wake up, sir knight! Wake *up*!'

My eyes snapped open and I sprang to my feet, drawing my sword as I did so.

There was the merchant, the whites of his terrified eyes glinting in the firelight. He was raving. 'It's out there!' he cried. 'It's out there!'

'*What's* out there?' I asked, placing a hand on his shoulder to steady him.

The merchant gripped my arm in both hands and drew his face close to mine. His forehead was drenched with sweat, his eyes were wide, his voice little more than a whisper.

'The dragon, of course,' he croaked.

*

Being bodyguard to a rich merchant was a
nice little earner for a knight down on
his luck. At least, that's what I'd thought three
weeks earlier when I was offered this job. I
should have known it wasn't going to be that
simple. It never is.

After all, I'm a free lance, a knight for hire. Trouble has a way of tracking me down, no matter how far I roam. This was no exception.

I was broke. Penniless as a juggler's monkey. And what was worse, I'd lost my squire, Wormrick.

I'd had to leave him nursing his broken leg beside a roaring fire in a fine inn. He had the last of my gold coins jingling in his pocket. It was the least I could do after our last little adventure.

That had started with yours truly doing a pretty duchess a favour. I'd agreed to retrieve a solid-gold drinking-vessel that had been "borrowed" by her wicked mother-in-law. It had ended with Wormrick being chased up a spiral staircase by a pack of castle hounds, and taking a nasty tumble from the top of a tall tower.

But that's another story...

So there I was, in a dusty city market down south. I had no squire, no money, and I needed a job – any job. But then, so did all the other knights down on their luck who had shown up in the market square that day.

I was just about to give up and retrieve Jed, my thoroughbred Arbuthnot grey, from the dingy stables where I'd left him that morning, when I spotted the merchant. He was tall, with a neatly clipped beard and expensive-looking clothes – flowing silken robes, purple turban, satin slippers. You know the type. As plump and gaudy as a stuffed peacock.

He'd rejected at least ten other knights before he got to me,

which wasn't surprising really, as they were even sorrier-looking than yours truly. Some were nursing old tournament injuries, while the others hadn't been in a tournament for years judging by their rusty armour and even rustier swordplay.

When it came to my turn, the Peacock glanced down at the sword at my side.

'Can you use that thing?' he said.

I drew the sword in a flash and cut the top off
the feather in his turban with a flick of my wrist.
He gawped at me, a look of astonishment on
his face.

'Impressive,' he said, as I returned my sword
to its sheath. 'You're hired.'

It turned out that he was a wealthy merchant.
He had a dozen mules loaded up with rolls of

fine silks, jars of
expensive oils and
sacks of fragrant
spices, and he needed to get
them from the city market to
his home town all in one
piece. That's where I came in.

'There are many dangers
along the way,' he said, his
voice hushed, his eyes narrowed. 'Brigands.
Wolves. And possibly worse...'

'I can handle most things...' I told him, trying
hard to sound nonchalant. I needed this job
and, judging by his clothes, this merchant looked
as if he could pay well. '...For the right price,'
I added.

The Peacock didn't bat an eyelid. 'Fifty gold
pieces if you get me and my merchandise to my
home town safely,' he announced.

It was a good offer, and I didn't think twice.
That's the problem. I never do.

'Done!' I said before he could change
his mind.

We set off bright and early the next morning. And as the sun rose higher, a low mist gave way to a bright, cloudless sky. The land grew drier and more desolate. Large scavenging birds with curved beaks and ragged wings wheeled across the sky as we left the city far behind us.

It became clear soon enough that the merchant was right about our route. There *were* brigands – though they were easy to spot, hanging around at crossroads and in the hills above mountain passes. Brigands aren't hard to avoid if you scout ahead and keep your eyes peeled, travel during the day and set up a secure camp at night. And the same goes for wolves, only with a good, bright campfire thrown in.

Of course, with a dozen heavily-laden mules and the Peacock on his skittish white mare, Jed and I couldn't relax for a moment. Back and forwards we went, to and fro, covering plenty of ground to make sure they all stayed safe. It was certainly tiring. Then again, compared to slaying monstrous hags and surviving blood-drenched tournaments, being a bodyguard to a rich merchant was easy.

A fortnight later, we came within a day's ride of our final destination. I could almost feel those fifty pieces of gold jangling in my pocket.

The sun had just slipped down beneath the horizon when I called a halt. Peacock wasn't happy. He wanted to press on through the night and get back home, which was understandable.

Understandable and foolish. Wolves liked nothing better than a night hunt, and we were in typical wolf country – a rocky, desolate plain, fringed with jagged mountains.

There was a chill wind blowing, which stirred up the dust and whistled between the boulders. It was spooky, but I was far too busy to let it bother me.

I had the mules to secure, Jed to settle, a fire to build, the torches to light, a meal to prepare... As ever, the Peacock said little and did even less.

Even so, I could tell that he wasn't happy. In fact he looked as nervous as a goose in a cook's kitchen. He flapped about anxiously as he tethered his skittish mare, Sherazah, to a rock. He was muttering under his breath and constantly looking over his shoulder.

'Something tells me you're not crazy about my choice of campsite,' I said to him later, as I served him up a portion of my Squire's Stew.

He shuddered and pulled his cape around him. 'This, my friend,' he said, 'is an evil place.'

'Evil place?' I said.

He nodded. 'The Plain of the Dead, it is called,' he said.

'Interesting name. Let me guess...' I said, stifling a smile. 'Now you're going to tell me why.'

2

'The Plain of the Dead,' the Peacock said, a tremor in his voice. 'It is well-named, my friend, believe me.'

I nodded, but said nothing.

'For it was here,' he went on, 'that a great battle took place. Many, many years ago,' he added thoughtfully, his eyes staring into mid-air. 'Before my father's father's father's time... A mighty battle. A *terrible* battle.'

The pair of us were seated on the ground beside the roaring campfire. I'd heard tales like this a hundred times before, tales to make the

hairs on the back of your neck stand on
end and your blood run cold. But that was all
they were; campfire tales, burning brightly in the
imagination at midnight, but a harmless heap of
ash by dawn.

'On that fateful day,' he continued, his dark
eyes glinting in the flickering firelight, 'two mighty
armies fought to the death on this rocky plain.
They stained the ground red with their blood.

Hordes from the
East, led by a
mighty Warrior
Lord with a
standard in
the shape of
a snarling
dragon in his
hands, attacked.
They fell upon the
army of the West,
their Golden Empress
at their head.'

'Sounds nasty,'
I said.

'As the heaps of the
slain grew all about, the Warrior Lord came face
to face with the Golden Empress.' He stared
deep into the flames of the campfire. 'And she
trembled at what she saw. The Warrior Lords'
face was the face of pure evil, eaten away by the
dark arts from which his power came.'

I nodded again. This was clearly not the first
time the Peacock had told his tale, and he knew
just when to pause for dramatic effect.

'For a moment, the din of the battle ceased,' he continued at last, his voice low and hushed. 'But only for a moment. As the sun cast its dying light across the bloodied plains, the Warrior Lord swung his curved sword and sliced the Golden 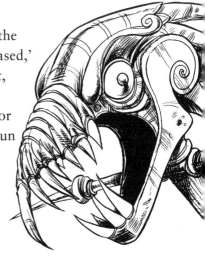 Empress's head from her shoulders, and cried out in triumph!'

The light from the campfire flames flickered across the merchant's face. From his brooding expression, I could tell the story wasn't over.

'The next instant, his cry of triumph turned to a howl of despair, as he looked down to find the Empress's dagger embedded in his chest, her dead hand still clasping its handle. As his life-blood mingled with those of the slain, the Warrior Lord planted his standard in the dusty ground and screamed out with his dying breath.

'"I claim this place for the forces of darkness, and evil shall dwell here ever after!"

'And with that he collapsed, the snarling dragon standard looming above his dead body. Ever since that time, this place has indeed been an accursed place.'

I nodded, and reached out to throw another piece of brushwood on the fire. But the merchant stayed my arm.

'The tale is not yet done,' he said, his voice trembling. 'It is said that, at the sound of his terrible curse, the snarling dragon from the standard sprang to life. It began to roam the battlefield, killing all those who were not already dead and feasting upon the corpses.'

Once again, although I nodded, I said nothing. It wouldn't be a campfire tale without a twist in the end, one to keep those hairs standing up on the back of the neck. Sure enough, it wasn't long in coming...

'What is more, my friend,' the merchant said, his expression deadly serious. 'Many believe that the dragon roams here still...'

'Uh-huh,' I said, throwing the brushwood on to the fire. It gave a satisfying crackle.

'Indeed,' he said. 'There are many who believe that the dragon must be appeased if it is not to roam farther afield and attack the unfortunate people of my poor home town.'

'You almost had me worried, there,' I said, patting him on the back and helping him to some more stew. 'If it weren't for one thing...'

'What's that?' he said, eyeing me suspiciously.

'I don't believe in dragons,' I said with a laugh.

It was the Peacock's turn to say nothing. Very slowly and deliberately, he wrapped his cape around him and raised the collar against the whistling wind. When he spoke, his voice was as cold as the night air itself.

'You should take heed, my friend,' he said.
'Just because you don't believe in something, it
doesn't mean it isn't there.'

I shrugged. 'I'll get back to you on that in the
morning,' I said, stoking up the fire so that it
would last through the night. As I did so, a
shower of bright orange sparks flew off into the
sky and I realized just how hard the wind was
now blowing. All round the plains, a mournful
howling rose and fell as it whistled through the
surrounding rocks and boulders.

It was certainly spooky out there. If I was
the superstitious type, I might almost have
found myself believing in evil warrior lords
and snarling dragons. Almost, but not quite.

The mules were all safely tethered,
Jed seemed fine and I certainly
wasn't going to let any
spooky stories spoil my
night's sleep. With the
fire blazing, hot and
bright, I lay down
and pulled the blanket
up round me.

Glancing round, I saw the Peacock doing the same.

I closed my eyes...

*

The next moment, there was someone beside me shouting my name.

'Wake up, sir knight! Wake *up*!'

3

Peacock had worked himself up into quite a state with his campfire tales of warrior lords and evil dragons. Now, he was dancing round the campfire, hopping from leg to leg. He claimed to have seen a dark shape prowling round our camp.

Mind you, dragons or no dragons, something had spooked the mules. They were jumping about like fleas in a frying-pan, tugging at their tethers and bellowing. And as for Jed, he was rolling his eyes and pawing the ground with his hoofs, froth bubbling from the corners of his mouth.

'Easy boy,' I said, stroking his muzzle and patting his neck. 'What is it, Jed? What's spooked you, eh?'

'It's the dragon!'
hissed the Peacock, brandishing a flaming log
from the fire. 'He knows it's out there. He can
sense it. They all can.'

'As I told you,' I said coldly, 'I don't believe in
dragons.'

'And as I told you,' he snapped back, 'just
because...'

'Yes, I remember what you said,' I broke in, pulling a tightly-bound brushwood torch dipped in tar from my belt. I lit it from the flaming branch Peacock was holding and strode out into the darkness. 'You settle those mules,' I called over my shoulder, 'while I scout round the camp.'

'Don't be long, sir knight,' babbled the Peacock. 'And please be careful!'

'Yes, yes,' I muttered, peering into the inky blackness.

These merchants, they're all the same. Hard as horseshoe nails when driving a bargain, but at the first hint of trouble, they go as soft as a princess's mattress, the lot of them!

Just then, from some way to my right, I heard a loud, high-pitched scream. I spun round. It was the Peacock. Something had certainly upset him.

'What is it?' I shouted over.

'Sherazah! My Sherazah! She's gone!'

I rushed over to him. Sure enough, at the end of the row of mules where the white mare had been tied up, there was nothing remaining but a short length of tether, snapped and frayed.

'Oh, Sherazah, where are you?' the Peacock bellowed into the night. His voice was lost in the wind that howled over the broad plain.

He turned to me, the look of panic in his face turning to sudden anger.

'I knew it was a mistake to camp here!' he shouted. 'And now my Sherazah is missing! This is all your fault, sir knight. You are the bodyguard, you must find her!'

I nodded curtly. I didn't need to be reminded of my duty, either as a bodyguard or as a knight. With my right hand, I drew my sword from its sheath with a soft, metallic *swoosh*; with my left hand I raised the burning torch. Then, without a word, I plunged into the darkness.

'I'll stay here and stand guard,' I heard the Peacock call after me.

When I glanced back, I saw that he had hurried to the safety of the campfire. I watched him for a moment, silhouetted against the leaping flames as he stoked the fire up higher and higher. He was clearly

determined that it would burn brightly enough to deter any passing creatures – real or imagined.

Turning away, I scanned the dusty ground around me for hoof-prints. There, some way off, I found curious tracks in the dust where something had recently been dragged across the ground. They stretched out before me, leading towards a rocky outcrop far ahead.

It wasn't looking too promising for the Peacock's precious mare. The creature that had made these tracks was big, and incredibly strong. If it was a wolf, it was the biggest wolf I'd ever come across. A lion, perhaps, or even some sort of bear? Whatever it was, the one thing I wasn't buying was the Peacock's dragon story.

The rocks and boulders came closer. They were laid out in strange, jagged formations. As I stared, they seemed to turn into hideous creatures with

fangs and claws and zigzag crests that ran the length of their spines...

I shook my head angrily from side to side. I was letting my imagination run away with me. Next thing you know, I'd be babbling on about dragons, just like the lily-livered Peacock. I rounded the rocks. The clouds cleared and the moonlight shone down, clear, bright and silvery white.

And that's when I saw it... The white horse.

It was slumped beside a boulder, in a pool of its own blood. Its neck had been torn open.

Keeping the burning
torch raised, I moved
forwards for a closer look.
As I did so, I heard a curious low, hissing
noise which seemed to come from the
shadows to my left. It grew louder for a
moment – and then was gone.

I drew closer still, and was suddenly
overwhelmed by a terrible gagging smell.
It wasn't only the poor creature's neck
which had been ripped open, but also
its belly, causing its guts to spill out all
over the ground. Whatever had got to
the Peacock's fine white mare, it had
certainly made a mess of it.

But one thing was for sure.
This wasn't the work of wolves. I'd
have heard a wolf pack yelping and
howling a mile off. No, whatever had
dragged the Peacock's horse away to this rocky
outcrop and torn it apart was far more powerful

and stealthy than any
wolf. What was
more, it seemed to
know just what it
was looking for.

I knelt down and removed the ornate gold bridle from the dead horse and slung it over my shoulder. Then, turning on my heels, I headed back to the camp. I didn't want to be around when whatever it was came back for a second helping. I found the Peacock hastily packing everything away. He clearly had no intention of spending the rest of the night in that godforsaken place.

'You read my mind,' I said, as I saddled up Jed. 'Let's get out of here. If we keep on through the night, we should make it to town by early morning.'

I handed the Peacock Sherazah's bridle.

'There was nothing I could do. Wolves got her,' I lied. The last thing I wanted was to spook him any more than he already was. 'You'll have to ride with me.'

We set off straight away. As we galloped across the desolate plain, the mules lumbering behind us, the clouds cleared once more and the full moon shone down. The Peacock must have

noticed it at once, because he leaned forwards in the saddle and hissed in my ear.

'You say wolves got my Sherazah, sir knight.' He gripped my sleeve tightly. 'Then tell me, why can't we hear them howling at the moon?'

4

We galloped through the night. Both of us were eager to put as much distance between ourselves and that terrible place as possible. The mules seemed as spooked as we were. A couple of times they threatened to break free of their guiding reins and stampede off into the night.

I whipped them into shape, ignoring the Peacock's protests to cut them loose. He clearly wasn't thinking straight. Despite his panic to get away though, I knew he'd thank me for saving his merchandise in the cold light of morning.

When it came, it certainly was a cold light, believe me. As we neared the Peacock's home town, pink rays were beginning to streak the sky to the east, accompanied by a half-hearted dawn chorus. The birds seemed unimpressed by their surroundings.

I knew just how they felt. The town was a dump.

As we approached, the Peacock jumped from the saddle and started pounding his fists on the gates of the town –

if you could call the ramshackle collection of
mud buildings a town, that is. Still, to the
Peacock, it was home and he certainly seemed
glad to be back.

'Open up!' he was bellowing, and hammered
on the gates loud enough to wake a pack of
stone-deaf wolfhounds. 'Open up, I say!'

Suddenly, there came the sound of a heavy
bolt being scraped back. Then, with a low creak,
the gates opened. I peered in. Several burly-
looking town guards in tattered chain-mail and
dented helmets were standing there, wiping sleep
from their eyes.

The Peacock seemed delighted to see them, because he collapsed into their arms. He gabbled excitedly about being attacked by a monstrous dragon and being practically eaten alive. To hear the Peacock tell it, you'd have thought we'd fought off this great winged, fire-breathing dragon with our bare hands. And that the bloodthirsty monster hot on our heels was intent on devouring every man, woman and child it could sink its drooling fangs into.

But the guards certainly bought it. The next thing I knew, they were running back through the streets, telling everyone they came across exactly what had happened to the merchant out on the plains that night.

The news spread like wildfire. By the time we reached the main square, there was a reception committee waiting for us. Townsfolk – young and old, and jabbering loudly – all clustered round the Peacock.

I left them to it. With a mouth dustier than a monk's cloister, and a thirst to match, I headed for the nearest inn. It was a shabby, rundown little joint – just like all the other buildings in this so-called town. But it was open for business, and that was all that mattered.

I pushed open the battered door and walked in. It was warm and dark inside. When my eyes had adjusted to the light, I strode up to the low table in the corner that seemed to serve as a bar, and ordered a tankard of ale. The landlord was a great bear of a man with tangled black hair and one thick eyebrow. He laughed at my request and pointed up at the goatskin gourds which hung from hooks in the rafters above him.

'You're not from round these parts, I take it, sir knight,' he said. 'You'll find no ale here. We have wine or water – and if I were you, I'd stick to the wine. It's cheaper.'

'Wine it is,' I said. 'And make it a large one.'

He nodded and produced a flagon the size of a bucket, and filled it from one of the gourds. 'Have this one on the house,' he said, handing me the flagon. 'You look as if you need it after the night you've had.'

45

Like I said, news travelled fast in this town.

I thanked him, raised the flagon to my lips and took a long draught. The golden liquid lit a fire from my throat to my belly. It had the kick of a mule and the taste of wet goat. But it washed away the dust in my mouth, so I wasn't complaining.

Taking the flagon with me, I crossed the warm, dark room to a rough-hewn table in the

corner. I sat down and stretched out my legs. It had been a long, hard night and a tiring two weeks on the road. I was exhausted. Now at last, I could put my feet up and relax. I took another swig from the flagon and sat back in my chair with a long sigh of contentment.

47

I should have known better, because at that moment, something I'd taken to be a heap of dusty rags in the opposite corner, suddenly let out a loud burp. I turned and found myself looking at a wrinkly, sallow-faced old man. He had thinning hair, threadbare clothes and dark, shifty eyes which peered out from beneath hooded lids. He clambered to his feet and came shuffling over.

I groaned. The last thing I wanted right now was company.

'Good morning, sir, knight,' came a whiny voice. 'I don't suppose you'd buy a little wine for a poor merchant down on his luck.'

I glanced over at the landlord.

'Pour him a drink,' I said, wearily.

The landlord tutted, but poured out another flagon of wine all the same.

'Thank you, sir knight,' said the old merchant. He grasped the flagon and gulped back its contents greedily. Then he wiped his mouth with a grimy hand and gave me a gap-toothed smile. 'Of course,' he said, settling himself down beside me, 'I wasn't always the poor wretch you see before you.' He turned his weaselly face towards me.

Here we go, I thought, another tavern sob-story of shattered dreams and disappointed hopes. I'd heard them all in my time. Sure enough, on his second flagon, the old merchant really got into his stride. He'd once been the wealthiest merchant in town. But then the big-city dealers swindled him, brigands stole his mules and the fire-breathing dragon out there ruined trade for everyone.

'This town's cursed,' he said, as he slurped his wine. 'Take my advice, sir knight, and get out while you still can. I would if I had any money.'

'Not before I pick up my pay,' I said, pushing back my chair and getting to my feet.

I was just about to leave, when the door flew open and in stepped a young woman. Even in this light, I could tell she was beautiful. Her hair was as black as ebony and her eyes were sapphire blue. The clothes she wore were as tattered and threadbare as the merchant's, but she was as dazzling as any princess in a jewelled gown.

Our eyes met and the strangest thing happened. My heart started beating faster than a squire's at his first tournament. My mouth became as dry as dust again. Something similar

51

must have been happening to her, because she stared back at me, a look of confusion playing over her beautiful face.

This is what happens when you drink the local wine, I thought, as I struggled to get a grip on myself. For a moment, I thought the Ragged Beauty was going to speak to me. Instead, she turned to old Heap-of-Rags at the table.

'Father!' she cried. 'When you didn't come home last night, I was so worried...' She rushed over to him. 'Still, no harm done, I suppose,' she added. 'So long as you're safe.'

The old man grunted and shrugged her hands from his shoulders.

'I've prepared you something for your breakfast with the last of the eggs in the house,' the Ragged Beauty went on. She smiled. 'Why don't you come back with me now, before it gets cold.'

The old man scowled. 'Why can't you just leave me alone!' he protested, getting to his feet. 'Can't a man have a quiet conversation without being pestered by his good-for-nothing daughter?'

I expected the Ragged Beauty to react to this, but instead she wiped a tear from her eye and turned away.

'I'm sorry I'm such a disappointment to you, father,' she said in a low voice.

'Oh, stop your snivelling and take me home!' snarled the ungrateful wretch. 'Or my eggs will be ruined.'

I wanted to box the old brute's ears for him, but I knew that would only upset his lovely daughter. So I stepped aside as they left, and waited for my head to clear and my heartbeat to return to normal.

I had to find the Peacock and sort out the little matter of my fifty gold pieces. I was just about to leave when who should walk in, but the very man himself.

'Ah, sir knight,' he said, standing beside me in the doorway. 'Just the person I was looking for.'

'Likewise,' I said, as we stepped out into the bright sunlight of the town square.

'We had a fortunate escape last night,' he said. 'Despite your foolish decision to make camp on the plains, even after my warnings...'

I said nothing. He could save his stories of dragons and ancient battles for those more gullible than myself.

'Still,' he continued, 'the mules all made it here in one piece, and my merchandise is safe. A job well done, sir knight. I am very pleased.' He pulled a pouch of gold coins from inside his robes and handed it over. 'I have, of course, had to dock a sum to cover the loss of my horse, Sherazah...'

I opened the purse and tipped the gold coins into my hand. There were ten missing.

Typical, I thought, as I returned them to the purse. They're all the same, these merchants...

'She was a very valuable horse, sir knight, as I'm sure you'll understand.'

It was clearly no use arguing with him. I smiled. Forty gold pieces was still a tidy sum. And not bad for a fortnight's work, I told myself. Not bad at all. It was the most money I'd held in my hand for a long time.

Looking up, I realized we were being watched. On the opposite side of the square, loitering in the shade, were two mean-looking, dust-covered characters with rusty armour and cheap swords. One of them had a mis-shapen helmet on his head, like a witch's cauldron. The other, I noticed when he smiled back at me, had crooked, gappy teeth.

Clearly they were itinerant swords-for-hire, down on their luck. I knew their type of course. They'd probably arrived in town on a job like mine, then stayed around just long enough to spend their money and get into trouble. One thing you could bet on in a little place like this, was that there would always be trouble. And it usually started with a pretty face in a tavern...

I thought of the Ragged Beauty and made up my mind, there and then, that it wasn't going to happen to me. Just as soon as I'd had a little bit of shut-eye, I was going to put as big a distance as possible between me and this flyblown town – Ragged Beauty or no Ragged Beauty.

*

I ended up taking a room above the inn. The landlord assured me he had the biggest, softest beds for rent. So, having stabled Jed round the back, I took him up on the offer.

He wasn't wrong.

I closed the shutters to cut out the glare of the morning sun. Then I kicked off my boots and threw myself down on the mattress. After two

weeks sleeping out on the baked earth plain, it
felt as soft as a feather-lined snowdrift. I was
asleep before my head hit the pillow.

The next thing I knew, I was woken up by the sound of loud music. Horns were blasting, drums were beating, cymbals were clashing. And on top of it all, was the sound of excited voices.

I climbed out of bed, went to the window and pushed the shutters open. The sun was low and orange. It seemed like I'd missed the entire day. Down below, the square was full of townsfolk, jostling and clamouring and craning their necks

to see the procession that was slowly making its way along the main street. It was a riotous affair, I can tell you.

I spotted several people I recognized from earlier that morning. It never takes long to get to know a new place. There were a couple of the city-guards. A bunch of shifty-looking itinerant knights. And there was the Peacock.

I frowned. He seemed to be speaking with...

But no, surely it couldn't be. I looked more closely. And yes, indeed. He was deep in conversation with old Heap-of-Rags.

Odd, I thought.

What happened next was even odder. I saw the Peacock slip the old merchant a small pouch.

Old Heap-of-Rags scuttled away, the money he'd just been given clutched in his bony hands. I knew there was only one place he could be heading – the inn, and for as much wine as he could guzzle.

But why, I wondered, had the Peacock been so generous? Given the way he'd docked my wages, I knew he wasn't the type to give his money away for nothing.

I returned my attention to the procession itself. Half the population of the city seemed to

have turned out to watch it, and they were all
surging forwards to the beat of the drums and
the clash of the cymbals. It was quite a party – if
that was what it was.

There were musicians and dancers, jugglers
and stilt-walkers, quite apart from the hundreds
of rowdy townsfolk keeping pace with them. I
looked back along the line of revellers winding
its way through the town. And there emerging
from round a corner I saw four hefty characters
dressed in black.

Hoisted up on their shoulders was a huge golden throne set upon two long poles. A princess, or maybe even a queen, sat upright and rigid as the throne swayed above the heads of the crowd. She was wearing shimmering purple robes, a broad silver turban and matching veil which hung down over her face. There were necklaces around her neck, bracelets at her wrists and ankles, and rings upon every finger. Each piece of jewellery was studded with multi-faceted stones that sparkled brightly in the low sunlight.

As she passed directly beneath my window, I gazed into the princess's eyes. I recognized them at once. Those large, clear eyes, like two sparkling sapphires. They belonged to the Ragged Beauty – but ragged no longer, for now she was dressed up in all the finery of a real princess.

But something was wrong. I could tell that from the instant our eyes met. There, showing plainly in those beautiful sapphire blue eyes, was fear and sheer, numbing panic.

'Help me!' she seemed to cry out to me with her eyes. 'Sweet sir knight, help me!'

5

Without a second thought, I grabbed my sword and was downstairs before the sound of the last cymbal had died away. I was making for the door when something caught my eye.

There, at a shadowy table in the back of the tavern, sat old Heap-of-Rags, a flagon of wine raised to his lips. A wave of rage overwhelmed me.

'Your daughter,' I cried out. 'Where are they taking her?'

'It's none of your business,' he slurred. 'She's gone for the good of the town...'

'Gone where?' I said.

'... For the good of the town...'

'What do you mean?' I demanded, grabbing
is filthy robes. 'What are they going to do to
er?'

'Good of the town,' he repeated, struggling to
ocus on me through bloodshot eyes. 'It's better
his way... I've got money now... To leave this
own... Start again...'

I stared back at the old man for a moment, my lip curling with revulsion, then let him go. He slumped back into the chair, his head lolling to one side. It was clear I wasn't going to get any more out of him. He let out a gurgling snore and his arm fell limply at his side, his fist unclenching as it did so. The Peacock's silver coins dropped down onto the floor at his feet.

That's how much his daughter means to him, I thought with disgust. I turned away and strode towards the door.

So, Peacock and the townsfolk had decided to stage a little party, with the Ragged Beauty as guest of honour – and paid her old wretch of a father for the privilege. By the look in her eyes, it was clear she wasn't too thrilled by the idea – and that's where yours truly came in. Like I said before, in small towns like this, trouble is always just around the next corner, and it looked like I'd just run into a whole heap of it.

Round at the stables, I found Jed had been fed, watered and brushed down – though the stable-boy who had looked after him was nowhere to be seen. I left some copper coins for his kindness, and a couple more for the

brushwood torches I took from a shelf. It was getting dark and I didn't want to be stuck out there in the plains without torch light.

I saddled up Jed, jumped onto his back and spurred him on. We passed through the deserted streets quickly. Then, as I steered us through the town gates, I saw the lights of the procession twinkling far ahead, winding its way along the rocky path towards the barren plain.

What could I, a single knight, do against a whole town? I thought bitterly.

Nevertheless, I followed them, taking care to stay far enough back to avoid being seen. Then, as they set off across the plain, I skirted round to the east. I kept myself concealed behind rocks and boulders, and remained upwind so that no one could hear Jed's hoof beats on the dusty

round – not that it was likely they'd have heard
nything above the deafening noise they were
till making.

   An hour or so later, I saw the procession come
  a halt. I dismounted, tied Jed up and crept
 loser for a better look. I'd take on the whole
 wn if so much as a single hair on the Ragged
 eauty's head was harmed, I vowed. I only
 oped, as I quietly drew my sword, that I
 ouldn't have to.

As the pipes and trumpets
blasted and the drums and
cymbals clashed, the four
hefty throne-carriers lowered their
load. Then one of them stepped forwards and
cut the ropes which, I now saw, had bound the
Ragged Beauty to the gold-painted chair. She was
pulled roughly to her feet.

Anger rose in my throat as she was bundled across to a tall, angular boulder. There, with her back to the rock, she was tied securely. I edged closer, my knuckles white as I gripped my sword.

This was it. I had the element of surprise on my side. I could take out two guards with my first sword blow, fell the third with a second cut, and drop the fourth with a dagger throw. That just left the rest of the town to tear me limb from limb for spoiling their little party. Still, if I could free Ragged Beauty and buy her enough time to escape while I went down fighting, then it would be worth it.

I was tensing every muscle in my body, about to leap out, when the strangest thing happened.

The music abruptly ceased, the voices fell still and the crowd turned on their heels. The Ragged Beauty was left, slumped and immobile. Muffled sobs racked her body, as the entire procession set off across the plain, back the way they had come.

The townsfolk looked shame-faced, embarrassed. Some of them stared down at their feet as they shuffled on. Yet, so far as I could see, none of them looked back. They were just leaving her there, all alone, tied to a rock on the barren plain.

I waited until the coast was clear, then stepped forward. As I approached, the Ragged Beauty looked up, her eyes wide with surprise above the silvery veil. I pulled it back, and saw an ugly gag across her beautiful mouth.

That's not all I saw. Up close, the clothes she had been dressed up in were cheap and tatty.

The sparkling jewels she wore were nothing but worthless brass and glass, cheap trinkets the lot of them.

What was going on? There was only one person who could tell me; the Ragged Beauty herself. I was reaching out to remove the gag when a gruff voice rang out behind me.

'Oi!' it bellowed. 'Not so fast!'

6

I spun round, to see two lowlife knights standing behind me. I recognized them at once. It was Cauldron Head and Snaggletooth, my old chums from the market square, with their rusty armour, their cheap swords and their envious glances.

They must have followed me, tracking me across the rocky plains. I cursed myself silently. I'd been careless; terribly careless. Intent on keeping track of the procession and wondering what to do when I caught up with it, I'd failed to notice that I was being tailed myself. Now I'd have to pay for my carelessness.

'Well, well, and what've we got here?' said Snaggletooth, grinning lop-sidedly. 'Quite the knight in shining armour, ain't we?' he sneered.

'Yeah,' leered his friend, Cauldron Head. 'Rescuing a fair damsel in distress... What a noble deed. We're impressed, sir knight.'

I said nothing. If these two ruffians had ever carried out a single knightly deed in their lives, then I'd snap my lance for firewood. Squires gone to the bad, most like. Petty thievery and moonlight ambushes were more their line of work.

Still, they were armed and dangerous, and I knew I couldn't afford to underestimate them.

Snaggletooth drew an evil-looking curved sword and waved it in my direction. Despite the

flecks of rust along
the blade, it looked as if it could do some
serious damage.

'Stand away from the wench,' he cried, 'and
hand over the purse we saw that stuck-up
merchant give you.'

'Yeah, cough up, and we'll make it nice and quick,' added Cauldron Head, drawing a finger menacingly across his throat. He pulled out a great two-handed broadsword, and grinned wickedly. 'Who knows?' he said. 'We might even let the girl go.'

'Nice offer, Fatso,' I said, drawing my own sword. I smiled. 'But I'm afraid if you want my money, you're going to have to work a bit harder to get it, you bloated bully-boy. And by the way, what *is* that on your head? Looks like a chamber pot...'

I saw a change come over Cauldron Head's expression. He was getting quite steamed up. Amazing what a bit of name-calling can achieve.

'This one's mine,' he snapped at Snaggletooth. 'Stand aside. I'll take care of him.'

Then, bellowing like a rutting bull, he lowered his head and charged at me. The great broadsword whistled through the air as he swung it above his head.

I let him get close to me – closer than the imbecile had any right to get – before stepping nimbly to one side. I deflected his heavy blow with a low counter-thrust of my own. Our swords clashed so hard that it sent judders of pain shooting up my arm from my wrist to my shoulder.

Cauldron Head roared with frustration. The great oaf had the strength of an ox, but he was heavy and lumbering, and slow on his feet.

I darted round to the left and lunged as he turned back to face me, slashing up and across with my sword. The tip of my blade made contact. In an instant, it traced an angry red line, beaded with blood, right the way across his cheek – and set him bellowing all the louder.

With a howl of animal rage, he raised his broadsword and brought it down with all his force. At that very moment, Snaggletooth stuck out a crafty leg and sent me sprawling. No doubt, he was trying to do his friend a favour. Instead, he saved my life.

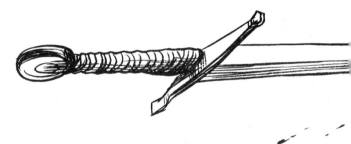

Cauldron Head's great broadsword – which would have split me in two from head to foot – crashed down on a boulder to my left. It was jarred from his grasp. This was my chance. I twisted round and threw my sword, like a dagger, straight at Snaggletooth's throat.

The razor-sharp blade flashed in the moonlight as it flew through the air in a smooth arc. Snaggletooth never stood a chance. It cut

through his leather breastplate like a hot knife
through butter and plunged deep into the base of
his neck.

I reached out, grasped Cauldron Head's broadsword from the dust and got to my feet to face him. An expression of confusion and dismay flashed across his face as he looked first at his friend, then at me.

'It's just you and me now, Potty-Hat,' I smiled.

Roaring like a wounded bear, Cauldron Head pulled the serrated knife from his belt and threw himself at me.

Instantly, I dropped to my knees, lowered my shoulders and braced the broadsword for impact.

Cauldron Head couldn't stop himself. The next instant, there was a loud *crunch* and a hideous *squelch* as the great lumbering oaf fell onto the blade and skewered himself. My shoulders jarred as they absorbed the impact through the broadsword.

looked up. Cauldron Head's face was inches
rom my own, a look of stupid surprise etched
 into his ugly features.

'*Urrgghh*!' he groaned softly as his eyes glazed over and blood-flecked drool dribbled down from the corners of his mouth.

With a grunt of effort, I pushed him aside. He slumped to the ground, his dead hands clutching the sword embedded in his chest.

I climbed to my feet wearily. It was just as I had thought. These two were no knights, with fighting skills forged on the tournament field and in dangerous quests. No, they were just a couple of jumped-up squires who had skipped sword-practice once too often – and now they'd paid the price.

Still, it was a high price to pay, and I hated being the one who'd had to collect it. Being a free lance knight could be a dirty business.

'Wffll mmffllmm!'

I turned round. The Ragged Beauty was still tied to the rock in her satin tat and tawdry finery. I walked over to her and untied her, removing the gag from her mouth as I did so. She struggled to get her breath between heartrending sobs, and when she did, her sapphire blue eyes flashed as they looked into mine.

'You're safe now,' I told her.

'But, sir knight,' she gasped, her voice trembling with emotion. 'I'm not. And neither are you...'

7

'What do you mean?' I said.

'We're both in terrible danger,' she cried, her face twisted with fear. 'We must leave this evil, godforsaken place at once!' She swallowed hard, and tears welled from the corners of her eyes. 'At once, sir knight! Do you hear me?'

I heard her loud and clear, but it made no sense.

'If you're worried about the townsfolk, I wouldn't be,' I reassured her. 'Judging by the way they were hurrying across the plain, they won't be back anytime soon.'

'It's not them,' she sobbed. 'It's this place. We must leave at once...'

'All right, all right,' I said calmly. She'd had a bad shock, I could see that. I'd have to go along with her fears, however silly they were. 'But where do you want to go?' I asked. 'Surely not back to the town...'

'No,' she said, her voice suddenly little more than a nervous whisper. 'No, I can't go back there. Not now...' She fell to her knees, the tears already streaming down her cheeks. 'Not after what they all did to me...'

I pulled a handkerchief from my back pocket

and held it out to her. She took it gratefully and dabbed it to her cheeks.

'I was the one chosen to be sacrificed,' she sobbed, her words cutting through the night air like a rapier. 'I begged my father not to, but... but... Oh, sir knight, he was only interested in the money...'

'Much good may it do him,' I growled. The old wretch had probably spent it all in the tavern by now.

'They always choose the poor ones,' she went on tearfully. 'It's never the rich merchants who offer up their daughters. And now...' She shook her head. 'I can never go back. Ever. If I did, they'd know that the dragon hasn't been appeased, and then... Oh, sir knight, I have nowhere else to go...'

As she spoke, everything slipped into place. The Peacock's wild story, the townsfolk hanging on his every word, and then the torchlit procession out onto this barren plain.

Of course! They actually believed that if they tied this poor girl to a rock and left her out here, then this imaginary dragon of theirs would leave them alone. If it hadn't been so cruel, it would have been laughable.

I smiled at the Ragged Beauty in her fake finery. No doubt, the townsfolk also believed the brass trinkets and glass baubles would attract this dragon of theirs, just as it's meant to in all the best fireside tales.

'Don't worry,' I said, as she dried those sapphire blue eyes of hers. 'I've seen my fair share of extraordinary things as a free lance, from weird hags to evil sorceresses. If there were such things as dragons, then I would have run across a few in my travels, believe me.' I laughed. 'Relax, Blue Eyes,' I said. 'This dragon of yours doesn't exist.'

'If it... d...doesn't, th... th... then...' she stammered, her eyes wide with terrible fear as she stared over my shoulder. 'Wh... wh... what is *that*?'

At that moment, a terrible stench filled the air, a mixture of bad eggs and rotting flesh. And from just behind me came a soft, wheezing hiss...

No, I thought, it couldn't be... Could it? There was only one way to find out. Gripping the handle of my sword with white-knuckled ferocity, I slowly turned around...

And wished that I hadn't. For there, facing me, was the most monstrous creature I had ever clapped eyes upon.

It had a long, knobbly body, four powerful
legs, and vicious-looking talons. Two evil,
bloodshot eyes stared out from its scaly face.
And when it opened its enormous fang-encrusted
jaws, the eye-watering stench of decay became a
hundred times stronger.

'*Kkhhhhhhhsss!*'

It let out a low, wheezing hiss. A grey forked tongue flicked in and out, in and out from between its dripping, yellow fangs, tasting the air. Its unblinking eyes stared right past me. I realized with a jolt that the monster had its gaze fixed on the Ragged Beauty.

Or rather, on the Ragged Beauty's neck.

Frozen to the spot with fear, she was unable to move so much as a muscle. I had to think fast.

'Your necklace,' I whispered to her.

'My n... n... necklace?' she stuttered back.

'Yes, quickly,' I told her. 'Give it to me now.'

She tore the great gaudy chain of sparkly glass jewels from her neck and held it out. I seized it at once, and waved it in front of the creature's face.

'Here you are, you great stinking brute!' I said in a soft, coaxing voice. 'You like these, don't you?' I continued as I backed away. 'Come on then. What are you waiting for?'

The creature swayed. Its bloodshot eyes looked from the necklace to the Ragged Beauty, and back again. It was as if it was trying to decide between her white flesh and the sparkly baubles in my hand. Its tongue flicked the air. Its talons scratched at the dusty ground.

Then, with a wheezing roar, it threw back its head, swung round and barrelled towards me.

I backed off as fast as I could, trying to lure the monster as far away from the Ragged Beauty as possible. And that's when it happened...

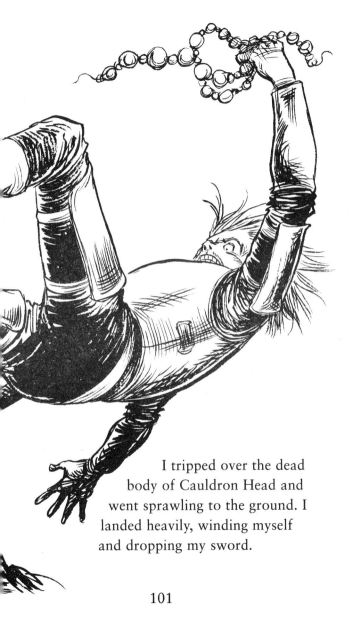

I tripped over the dead
body of Cauldron Head and
went sprawling to the ground. I
landed heavily, winding myself
and dropping my sword.

The monster saw its chance. With a deafening roar, it leapt at me and seized my left arm – the one clutching the necklace – in its massive jaws. I swear that if it hadn't been for my armour, it would have bitten clean through my arm right then and there. As it was, I was held fast by the creature's vice-like grip.

Desperate to get hold of the sparkling necklace, the creature began shaking its massive head violently from side to side, tossing me about like a rag doll.

The last thing I remember was a large boulder
embedded in the rocky plain coming up to
meet me.

Then blackness...

When I came to, I was being dragged across the rocky ground, the monster still clutching my arm in its jaws, like a starved castle-hound with a banquet bone. There was only one thing for it. I did what I always do in hopeless situations like this.

I played dead.

Through the dust and darkness ahead, I could just make out a small opening in the rock-strewn landscape. The monster was making straight for it. It lumbered through the narrow crevice – knocking me against the sides of the wall as it did so – and down into its foul-smelling den.

There, it proceeded to shake me around again until, my cold "dead" hands allowed the necklace to fall from their grasp.

Satisfied for a moment, the monster spat me out. I rolled into the corner and continued playing dead for all I was worth, while it snuffled and drooled disgustingly over the worthless trinket.

I opened one eye. There was a shaft of moonlight cutting down through the air into the terrible underground lair from above.

In the sombre gloom, I saw the monster toss the necklace to one side with its muzzle, and turn towards me with an evil hiss. I let out a groan of despair. It had had the starter, now it wanted the main course, and without my sword, I knew that there was nothing I could do to protect myself.

So this was it, I thought bitterly. This was how I was to meet my end, as a banquet for a dragon.

And I had thought it was just a local superstition! I should have paid more attention to the Peacock's campfire tale. There's always *some* truth in that kind of story.

Of course, it was the word "dragon" that was to blame. To me, dragons belonged in far-fetched tales, where they had wings and forked tails and

fiery breath. They weren't real. Not like the
creature looming up before me now. But I had to
admit, as it opened its massive jaws, "dragon"
seemed as good a name as any for the loathsome
monster. And as for its breath...

I slowly got to my feet and clenched my fists. If I was about to be devoured, I decided, then I'd do my very best to stick in the monster's throat. With a stinking roar of anger, the dragon came barrelling towards me.

8

Then all at once and without any warning, the shaft of light penetrating the underground lair was blocked out.

'Sir knight! Sir knight!' someone called from above.

It was the Ragged Beauty.

The monster hesitated for a moment at the sound of her voice.

'Quick, take this!' she shouted, and the next moment I heard something clattering down by my side. I reached out desperately, and my fumbling hand closed round the handle of my sword. And not a moment too soon, for the monster lunged at me, its jaws gaping so wide, I swear I could see the remains of its last feast.

'Eat this, dragon breath!' I roared, as I thrust my sword deep into its gaping maw. There was a grinding, and a crunching, and a squelching as I drove the blade deeper. Through its gullet it went, its gizzard and down its gaping throat until, with my arm buried almost up to the shoulder, I pierced the monster's black heart.

A rush of blood and bile drenched me and the stench was overpowering. Gagging for breath I pulled my sword back out of the great, dying monster, which collapsed on to the cavern floor. Soon it lay still, its ancient body lifeless at last.

I looked up to see the Ragged Beauty climbing down through the cave entrance to join me.

'Oh, sir knight,' she exclaimed. 'I can't tell you how grateful I am.'

You could try, I thought.

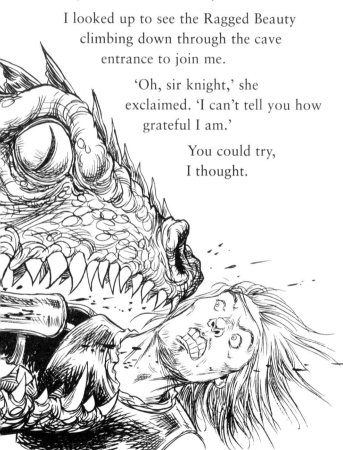

'I'm forever in your debt, sir knight. Tell me how I can repay you and I shall do so, I swear...'

This was more like it. 'Oh, it was nothing,' I said modestly. 'All in a day's work for a free lance.'

I pulled one of the pitch-tipped torches from my belt. 'Now let's throw some light on the matter,' I said.

I struck my
flints, and the
sparks ignited the dry
torch, which crackled into
flames. The brightness illuminated
the entire cavern.

The Ragged Beauty gasped. I didn't blame her,
for all round us was a scene of almost
unimaginable horror. The dead creature itself
was sprawled out over the floor, blood and bile
soaking into the dust. Close to, it looked even
older than I had imagined. Lines and welts and
jagged scars decorated its stinking body.

Just how long had this ancient beast lurked
here? I wondered.

The answer lay all about me, in the form of the bones of its countless victims – victims that must have stretched back through the centuries. I staggered backwards, crunching on the crumbling bones beneath my feet.

Large bones, small bones. Thigh bones, thumb bones, hip and finger bones; some still connected to their neighbours, some long since separated. Ribs and spines, and papery skulls, their empty yellowed eye-sockets staring back at me. It was as though I'd tumbled down into a long-forgotten crypt. And there, within this gruesome collection, sparkling in the torchlight, were the tatty glass trinkets and baubles that the sacrificed victims had been adorned with.

'Come, sir knight,' said the Ragged Beauty. 'Let us leave this terrible place at once.'

I nodded
and was about to follow her, when something
caught my eye. Taking the Ragged Beauty's hand,
I ventured deeper into the dragon's lair.

I raised my flaming torch up high. And to my
astonishment, there among the most ancient of
the dragon's victims, was a glittering, glinting,
gleaming treasure trove beyond my wildest
dreams.

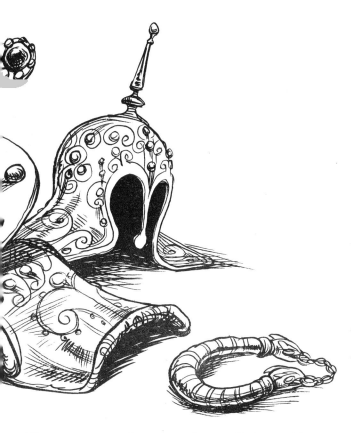

There were jewel-encrusted swordbelts, gold breastplates, amulets of hammered silver and half-crushed helmets of finest gold, studded with precious stones... And at the centre, sticking up from the heap of priceless items, was a single item more startling than all the rest.

It was a gold standard, adorned with precious stones, which had a snarling dragon at one end – and a skeletal hand still clasping it, the bone splintered at the elbow, at the other. Close by lay a shattered rib-cage with a golden dagger still embedded between the curved bones.

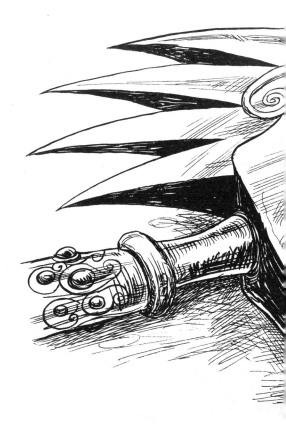

The Peacock's story came flooding back to me. It was true, all of it.

I had dismissed it, and yet here was the evidence of that mighty battle all around us. Beside me, I could feel the Ragged Beauty tremble.

'Please, please, sir knight,' she said, her voice low and frightened. 'I cannot bear to remain in this terrible place a moment longer.'

She had a point. The whole place reeked of death and decay. But before we left it far behind us, like a bad dream brought on by a campfire tale, there was one last thing I had to do.

*

As the sun rose on a bright new day, I spurred Jed on. He increased his pace and, for a moment, the leading rein between us and the two scruffy horses of Snaggletooth and Cauldron Head went taut.

I turned to check that the precious burdens upon their back were still securely in place. And as I did so, my cheek brushed against the beautiful, dark hair of the Ragged Beauty, who was behind me in the saddle, her arms wrapped tightly around my waist. She was fast asleep, and had been so for the last hour, but there was a little smile playing on her lips.

It had taken me more than a couple of trips down into the evil lair to gather up every bit of the dragon's hoard. It now clinked and clunked on the backs of the horses.

As we rode north, away from that accursed plain, I tried to picture the scene all those years ago. A hideous carrion-eating lizard, attracted by the smell of death drifting on the cold wind, waddled across the rocky plain from some far off swamp or muddy riverbank. It must have hardly been able to believe its luck when it reached that blood-soaked battlefield.

All those corpses. All those sparkling jewels. No wonder it had taken up residence in a cosy cave close by, where it could drag the carcasses and devour the flesh in peace. And as the bones had piled up, so the gold and the jewels had accumulated unseen, and the lizard had grown to a monstrous size.

Little wonder that the legend had arisen. Terrified shepherds and passing merchants must have stumbled back to the town to report of the dragon they had seen.

Of course, the creature had been forced to become bolder when the source of food had dried up. Unwilling to abandon its glittering hoard of treasure, it had remained in its lair. Only now it emerged to attack sleepers round campfires, rather than the corpses of the slain. Over the years, the terrified townsfolk must have learnt that feeding it victims kept the rest of them safe, so they found people to sacrifice.

The poor. The weak. The vulnerable... Isn't that always the way?

I felt the Ragged Beauty shifting in the saddle behind me. She was safe now, and the Peacock and his fellow townsfolk would slowly realize, after a year or two, that they were safe, too. Not that either of us cared. No, we were leaving it all behind us.

I smiled. I had enough gold to set myself up in a fine castle as a lord, and the Ragged Beauty had agreed to become my lady.

And as for Wormrick, he would become a fine knight. With my new-found wealth, I'd see to that. Not for him the shiftless, uncertain life of a free lance. No, when Wormrick earned his spurs, he would become a bonded knight serving a rich lord, who would take pride in his triumphs and honour his fine deeds.

And who would be that rich lord? Why, none other than yours truly.

Don't get me wrong. I'd loved the life of a free lance, but neither Jed nor I was getting any younger. Now I had wealth beyond my wildest dreams and, more precious by far, the love of a fine woman. As I rode towards the rising sun, I knew that my free lance days were behind me for ever.

It had been a good life, but the best was still to come.

THE END